CW00458068

The REAL STAR
of Bethlehem

The REAL STAR
of Bethlehem

HOW THE TRUTH OF THE NATIVITY
STORY EXCEEDS THE MYTHS

ARTHUR FRANCIS GREEN

Sovereign World

Published by Sovereign World Ltd
PO Box 784
Ellel
Lancaster
LA1 9DA
United Kingdom

www.sovereignworld.com
Twitter: @sovereignworld
Facebook: www.facebook.com/sovereignworld

ISBN: 978 1 85240 712 4

Printed in the United Kingdom
Editing by Sheila Jacobs
Front cover design by David Lund
Cover image licensed by GoodSalt Inc.

To the greater glory of God and His Holy Word
and
To my dear wife, Jill
whose loyal and unwavering support has
enabled this book to be written

Contents

Acknowledgments

I would especially like to acknowledge the contribution to my Biblical education made by Dr Don Hender of Bournemouth, England. His invaluable teaching and mentoring over many years have broadened and extended my understanding of Scripture and the living faith of Christ.

I offer my grateful thanks to my wife and children for their efforts in proofreading the text, not only for errors, but also for readability and consistency.

There are many other people, too numerous to mention, who, over the years, have helped me to develop my understanding of Scripture. I offer my heartfelt gratitude for their invaluable support and fellowship.

Last but not least, I would like to acknowledge the kindness and support of the publishing team at Sovereign World in bringing this small book to fruition.

Finally, I am responsible for any and all errors within these pages. My greatest wish is that, under God's grace, the reader will accept the good and reject any unwitting errors.

Arthur F. Green
Ferndown
August 2012

We Three Kings – Traditional Christmas Carol

1. We three kings of Orient are
Bearing gifts we traverse afar
Field and fountain, moor and mountain
Following yonder star
CHORUS
O Star of wonder, star of night
Star with royal beauty bright
Westward leading, still proceeding
Guide us to thy Perfect Light

2. Born a King on Bethlehem's plain
Gold I bring to crown Him again
King forever, ceasing never
Over us all to reign
CHORUS

3. Frankincense to offer have I
Incense owns a Deity nigh
Prayer and praising, all men raising
Worship Him, God most high
CHORUS

4. Myrrh is mine, its bitter perfume
Breathes a life of gathering gloom
Sorrowing, sighing, bleeding, dying
Sealed in the stone-cold tomb
CHORUS

5. Glorious now behold Him arise
King and God and Sacrifice
Alleluia, Alleluia
Earth to heav'n replies
CHORUS

Rev. John Henry Hopkins (1820–91)

Prologue

Misconceptions

When we sing Christmas carols and remember the birth of our Saviour, one carol always sung among the favourites is "We Three Kings of Orient Are …" It is quite descriptive of the events of the Magi, coming from the East with gifts for the Messiah, following "yonder star". It is also poetry and expresses a great deal of information in a few lines of verse. Calling the Magi "kings" in the title and first line of the carol is misleading, but the idea of earthly kings coming to honour *the* King is almost irresistible. "Magi" means "Wise Men" or "Learned Men". Included in their learning would be astronomy and astrology – something that has been emphasized over the years to the point of caricature. Also, when we look at the traditional iconography of Christmas, these so-called kings arrive at the stable with the shepherds at the same time. We are used to seeing the tableau of the Nativity scene: a stable with a manger (an animal's eating trough), with some animals round about; Joseph, Mary and Jesus in the centre; the three "kings" with their gifts; the shepherds crowding in. All are looking at the infant Jesus in the manger, and the Star is shining above the whole scene.

We can understand why it is depicted this way, because the focus of everything is on the birth of the Messiah – the birth of Jesus is the most significant event in the history of the world and we should rightly give it the very highest importance. So we see in our art, and in almost all depictions of the Nativity, that everything is present all at once, and all are adoring the Messiah, who is naturally placed at the centre of the scene. Unfortunately, this is misleading in some significant ways, even though the basic facts are there. It all combines into a certain homely pastiche, and obscures the real point of the story of the Star of Bethlehem.

The traditional images we see of the Magi and the shepherds visiting the stable where Jesus was born, together with the Star, and all at the same time, are wrong. It is no doubt splendid iconography and a useful aid in retelling the story of the Nativity, but it has pulled together two separate events into one image, as the accounts in Luke and Matthew will show when we look at them. This can and does add to the confusion about the Star.

In this small book I hope to explain both the nature and the significance of the Star of Bethlehem. It is often overlooked, and relegated to a mere prop in the stage scenery. I hope to show that the Real Star of Bethlehem is a major part of the story; by neglecting it we miss a tremendous message from the one true and Living God, who is the same yesterday, today and tomorrow.

1

Is the Star Genuine?

NATURALISTIC EXPLANATIONS

Modern scientists and philosophers and even many theologians try to find a naturalistic explanation for the miracles of the Holy Bible. The Biblical story of the Nativity and the Star of Bethlehem is no exception.

There are various attempts at giving a natural explanation for the Star, such as a supernova, or a comet, or a planetary conjunction. Actually, none of these explanations is very satisfactory; and they are at best very strained attempts to harmonize natural events with the Biblical accounts. One of the main problems is that the timing of all these proposed astronomical events cannot be properly aligned with the date of birth of Our Lord Jesus Christ.

Since the timing is a problem, the conclusion is made that the Star cannot be real, because it cannot be explained by these natural events. Therefore the

3

Star is just a piece of colourful fiction – another Biblical myth. This attitude, that if there is no natural explanation it must be unreal or mythical, also creeps over into the question of Jesus Himself: if the Star is a myth, is He real? And so many people have come to doubt the existence of Jesus, and the reality of the Gospel narratives, which include the Star of Bethlehem as part of the Nativity.

However, so much emphasis has been placed on the assumption that it must be something like that, that we have all become infected with the idea, and are casting around for an explanation. Atheists and others don't have a problem, because to them the Bible is a heap of myths anyway. It is Christians who have the biggest problem; especially those who take the Bible very seriously as the inerrant Word of God. Why would God allow something that wasn't true to become part of His Word?

Well, we don't need to start from the point of view that everything must have a natural explanation. The birth of Christ is a supernatural event and is not subject to naturalistic thinking. The modern attitude of scientists and philosophers can be set to one side, as we begin to think about the supernatural events of the Nativity and the Star. You will have noticed that I have capitalized the word "Star". You will see why later.

LITERARY INVENTION

We need to take a look at another attempt at an explanation – that is, the Star is a literary invention. Many important scholars regard the Star as a literary invention of the author of the Gospel of Matthew, to claim fulfilment of an Old Testament prophecy:

I see Him, but not now;
I behold Him, but not near;
A Star shall come out of Jacob;
A Scepter shall rise out of Israel,
And batter the brow of Moab,
And destroy all the sons of tumult.

(Numbers 24:17)

In the book of Numbers, the word "Star" is capitalized because it is referring to the Messiah, the coming Ruler of Israel. This has become known as the Star Prophecy. It also aligns with another Old Testament prophecy which is important to our story:

But you, Bethlehem Ephrathah,
Though you are little among the thousands of Judah,
Yet out of you shall come forth to Me
The One to be Ruler in Israel,
Whose goings forth are from of old,
From everlasting.

(Micah 5:2)

There is no doubt; both of these prophecies refer to the person of the coming Messiah, whom we know as Jesus Christ. Respectively, these were written about 1,400 and 700 years before Christ. In the historical sense they are truly prophetic, but they should not be taken out of context and forced to refer to the Star of Bethlehem recorded in Matthew's Gospel. Because of this confusion of the Star and the Messiah, many respected scholars looking for more substantial evidence soon became disillusioned and concluded that the Star was a later invention, there to make a point about the birth of important people. The ancients believed that astronomical events were connected to earthly events. Astrological and astronomical signs were routinely associated with the birth of important people, such as kings, the birth of new dynasties, and Greek and Roman heroes. It was in this way that Origen (AD 185–254), one of the most influential early Christian theologians, in his refutation of Celsus, a pagan philosopher who made strong criticisms of Christianity, connected the Star Prophecy with the Star of Bethlehem:

It has been observed that, on the occurrence of great events, and of mighty changes in terrestrial things, such stars are wont to appear, indicating either the removal of dynasties or the breaking out of wars, or the happening of such circumstances as may cause commotions upon the earth. But we have read in the *Treatise on Comets* by Chæremon the Stoic that on some occasions also, when good was to happen, comets made their appearance; and he gives an account of such instances. If, then, at the commencement of new dynasties, or on the occasion of other important events, there arises a comet so called, or any similar celestial body, why should it be matter of wonder that at the birth of Him who was to introduce a new doctrine to the human race, and to make known His teaching not only to Jews, but also to Greeks, and to many of the barbarous nations besides, a star should have arisen? Now I would say, that with respect to comets there is no prophecy in circulation to the effect that such and such a comet was to arise in connection with a particular kingdom or a particular time; but with respect to the appearance of a star at the birth of Jesus there is a prophecy of Balaam recorded by Moses to this effect: "There shall arise a star out of Jacob, and a man shall rise up out of Israel."[1]

As we have already noted, the "star out of Jacob" figuratively refers to the Messiah Himself and not to a real astronomical body. At the time of Christ it had already become widely seen as a reference to the coming of the Messiah. Unfortunately, since the time of Origen, the Star of Bethlehem has been traditionally linked to the Star Prophecy and confused with an astronomical event. It is easy to see why later scholars were looking for astronomical signs at the time of Jesus' birth. None could be made to fit satisfactorily, and so the Star of Bethlehem has been widely dismissed as a literary invention or a "pious fiction".

On the other hand, while Origen argued for an astronomical explanation, John Chrysostom (AD 347–407) viewed the star as purely miraculous:

For if ye can learn what the star was, and of what kind, and whether it were one of the common stars, or new and unlike the rest, and whether it was a star by nature or a star in appearance only, we shall easily know the other things also. Whence then will these points be manifest? From the very things that are written. Thus, that

---

[1] Origen, *Contra Celsum*, Book I, Chapter LIX http://www.ccel.org/ccel/schaff/anf04.vi.ix.i.lx.html.

this star was not of the common sort, or rather not a star at all, as it seems at least to me, but some invisible power transformed into this appearance, is in the first place evident from its very course ... How then, tell me, did the star point out a spot so confined, just the space of a manger and shed, unless it left that height and came down, and stood over the very head of the young child? And at this the evangelist was hinting when he said, "Lo, the star went before them, till it came and stood over where the young Child was."[2]

So we can see that the debate about the nature of the Star has been going on for a long time! It's not just a modern problem; this is a centuries-old discussion. What do *you* think? For my part, as will become clear later, I agree with John Chrysostom, that the very description of the Star and its activities rules out a naturalistic explanation – but what is this "invisible power" he mentions? We shall investigate this as we go on, and we shall discover the tremendous message behind the Star of Bethlehem.

Also, Chrysostom states that we can know "From the very things that are written." He is, of course, referring to the Bible accounts, and to these we must now turn.

---

[2] John Chrysostom, *Homilies on the Gospel of St Matthew*, Homily VI http://www.synaxis.org/cf/volume19/ECF00002.htm.

2

The Truth of
the Bible Accounts

So, how can we know what the Bible says is true?
Well, we can know something by one of three ways:

1. *Our Own Witness.* We were there; we saw; we heard;
   we bear witness to the truth of the event. This
   applies to recent events within our own lifetime.

2. *By Authority.* We trust someone who tells us; who was
   there and can bear witness. This applies to events
   that occurred within living memory of all those still
   alive, who were there at the time.

3. *By Credible Historical Evidence.* This is usually in
   written form and gives the accounts of people long
   dead. They were there and they wrote down what
   they saw and heard. Usually there will be more than
   one independent account, lending a high degree of
   credibility to the historical record.

Clearly, the events of the Nativity and the Star are so far
in the past that we are only left with the third option:

credible historical evidence. We know that the Bible is a credible historical document, since archaeology is constantly finding things that confirm its historical accuracy. So we can trust it, and we can trust the truth of the eyewitnesses who wrote down what they saw and heard. What they report to us, across the centuries, is that Jesus was born of Mary, in the town of Bethlehem, according to the prophecies of the Old Testament. Shepherds in the hills around Bethlehem also saw the Glory of God, many angels and the whole host of heaven, singing praises to God about this earth-shattering event. Afterwards, they went to the stable in Bethlehem to see for themselves, and then reported what they had seen to everyone around.

The Bible also records that, about a year after His birth, Magi, or Wise Men, arrived from the East, having followed the sighting of a Star. What they probably saw to inspire such an arduous journey was a different manifestation of the Glory of the Lord as He appeared to the shepherds. To the Magi He appeared as a leading Star. Eventually they were led to Jesus' home, where they gave gifts of gold, frankincense and myrrh.

The Bible is actually a very straightforward documentary record of the events. When we read the two Biblical accounts in full, we shall see that both begin by placing the events they describe firmly into historical context:

Luke writes:

And it came to pass in those days that a decree went out from Caesar Augustus that all the world should be registered. This census first took place while Quirinius was governing Syria.

(Luke 2:1–2)

Matthew writes:

> Now after Jesus was born in Bethlehem of Judea
> in the days of Herod the king ...
>
> (Matthew 2:1)

Matthew was writing from the Jewish point of view, and Luke from the wider context of the Graeco-Roman world. Both are historically correct. There have been some suggestions that Luke got it wrong about the census and the timing of Quirinius' governorship, but these have been convincingly refuted by the available documentary and archaeological evidence. We can also trust the balance of these accounts as truthful written testimony, taken down from eyewitness statements of the events surrounding the birth of Jesus. So let's start from the point of view that the Biblical accounts are correct in all their details and these things really happened. What are we to think? Well, let's read what the Bible says. Here are the Biblical accounts of Luke and Matthew.

LUKE 2:1–24

And it came to pass in those days that a decree went out from Caesar Augustus that all the world should be registered. This census first took place while Quirinius was governing Syria. So all went to be registered, everyone to his own city.

Joseph also went up from Galilee, out of the city of Nazareth, into Judea, to the city of David, which is called Bethlehem, because he was of the house and lineage of David, to be registered with Mary, his betrothed wife, who was with child. So it was, that while they were there, the days were completed for her to be delivered. And she brought forth her firstborn Son, and wrapped Him in swaddling cloths, and laid Him in a manger, because there was no room for them in the inn.

Now there were in the same country shepherds living out in the fields, keeping watch over their flock by night. And behold, an angel of the Lord stood before them, and the glory of the Lord shone around them, and they were greatly afraid. Then the angel said to them, "Do not be afraid, for behold, I bring you good tidings of great joy which will be to all people. For there is born to you this day in the city of David a Savior, who is Christ the Lord. And this will be the sign to you: You will find a Babe wrapped in swaddling cloths, lying in a manger."

And suddenly there was with the angel a multitude of the heavenly host praising God and saying:

"Glory to God in the highest,

And on earth peace, goodwill toward men!"

So it was, when the angels had gone away from them into heaven, that the shepherds said to one another, "Let us now go to Bethlehem and see this thing that has come to pass, which the Lord has made known to us." And they came with haste and found Mary and Joseph, and the Babe lying in a manger. Now when they had seen Him, they made widely known the saying which was told them concerning this Child. And all those who heard it marveled at those things which were told them by the shepherds. But Mary kept all these things and pondered them in her heart. Then the shepherds returned, glorifying and praising God for all the things that they had heard and seen, as it was told them.

And when eight days were completed for the circumcision of the Child, His name was called JESUS, the name given by the angel before He was conceived in the womb.

Now when the days of her purification according to the law of Moses were completed, they brought Him to Jerusalem to present Him to the Lord (as it is written in the law of the Lord, "Every male who opens the womb shall be called holy to the LORD"), and to offer a sacrifice according to what is said in the law of the Lord, "A pair of turtledoves or two young pigeons."

MATTHEW 2:1–16

Now after Jesus was born in Bethlehem of Judea in the days of Herod the king, behold, wise men from the East came to Jerusalem, saying, "Where is He who has been born King of the Jews? For we have seen His star in the East and have come to worship Him."

When Herod the king heard this, he was troubled, and all Jerusalem with him. And when he had gathered all the chief priests and scribes of the people together, he inquired of them where the Christ was to be born.

So they said to him, "In Bethlehem of Judea, for thus it is written by the prophet:

'But you, Bethlehem, in the land of Judah,
Are not the least among the rulers of Judah;
For out of you shall come a Ruler
Who will shepherd My people Israel.'"

Then Herod, when he had secretly called the wise men, determined from them what time the star appeared. And he sent them to Bethlehem and said, "Go and search carefully for the young Child, and when you have found Him, bring back word to me, that I may come and worship Him also."

When they heard the king, they departed; and behold, the star which they had seen in the East went before them, till it came and stood over where the young Child was. When they saw the star, they rejoiced with exceedingly great joy. And when they had come into the house, they saw the young Child with Mary His mother, and fell down and worshiped Him. And when they had opened their treasures, they presented gifts to Him: gold, frankincense, and myrrh.

Then, being divinely warned in a dream that they should not return to Herod, they departed for their own country another way.

Now when they had departed, behold, an angel of the Lord appeared to Joseph in a dream, saying, "Arise, take the young Child and His mother, flee to Egypt, and stay there until I bring you word; for Herod will seek the young Child to destroy Him."

When he arose, he took the young Child and His mother by night and departed for Egypt, and was there until the death of Herod, that it might be fulfilled which was spoken by the Lord through the prophet, saying, "Out of Egypt I called My Son."

Then Herod, when he saw that he was deceived by the wise men, was exceedingly angry; and he sent forth and put to death all the male children who were in Bethlehem and in all its districts, from two years old and under, according to the time which he had determined from the wise men.

Although Luke's account comes after Matthew in the New Testament, Luke is describing the events of Jesus' birth, whereas Matthew begins: "Now *after* Jesus was born in Bethlehem …" (italics mine). I have placed the accounts in chronological order so that we can better follow the events and understand what the Star is, what it does, and what is its real significance.

We are told that, at the time of the birth of Jesus, Wise Men saw it from the East, from a long way off, and so came towards the West to find the prophesied Messiah, the King of the Jews. In ancient times this was a long and difficult journey and would take many months; the preparation for the journey would also take weeks, if not months. By the time they arrived, possibly up to a year later, Jesus would have been taken to a proper home, probably with relatives, since Bethlehem was the hometown of his parents. He would no longer be in the stable with the animals. Not only would the census be over, but the festival pilgrims would have gone home, and finding a place to stay until the Child was old enough to travel would no longer be a problem.

Finally, when the Magi stated "For we have seen His star in the East …" a better translation of the New Testament Greek would be "For we have seen His star at its rising" or possibly "when it arose". *Thayer's Greek-English Lexicon* explains that the Greek words for "rising" and "setting" were used to denote East and

West respectively, because of the common usage for the rising and setting of the sun. So "rising" became synonymous with "East" and "setting" with "West".

Adam Clarke's Commentary for Matthew 2:2 has these two statements:

- [In the east] Εν τεε ανατολεε (pronounced: en tee anatolee), At its rise.

- ανατολη (anatolee) rising; and δυσμη (dusmee) setting; are used in the New Testament for east and west.[3]

So we can conclude that the Magi saw the Star when it first appeared, or "at its rise". Can we deduce when this was? Yes, we can – from Luke's account:

> And behold, an angel of the Lord stood before them, and the glory of the Lord shone around them ...
>
> (Luke 2:9)

This was exactly at the birth of Christ, when the glory of the Lord first shone around the shepherds at Bethlehem. The Greek word for "star" simply means "radiance" or "brilliance". Appearing in the form of a great light or brilliance at the birth of Jesus, it is the sudden appearance of the Glory of the Lord that is

---

[3] Adam Clarke, The Holy Bible, Containing the Old and New Testaments ... With a Commentary and Critical Notes; Designed as a Help to a Better Understanding of the Sacred Writings (London: Thomas Tegg, 1832), vol. V, p. 44; copy in author's possession. (Comments in brackets are mine.)

the only explanation for the Star of Bethlehem and what the Magi saw. Of course the Star subsequently appeared as a supernatural signpost to the Magi on their long journey, and so must have shone day and night. John Chrysostom again:

> For it appears not in the night, but in mid-day, while the sun is shining; and this is not within the power of a star, nay not of the moon; for the moon that so much surpasses all, when the beams of the sun appear, straightaway hides herself, and vanishes away. But this by the excess of its own splendour overcame even the beams of the sun, appearing brighter than they, and in so much light shining out more illustriously.[4]

Another strange property of the Star was the appearing and guiding, then hiding and reappearing again, then ultimately vanishing. On their way to Jerusalem, the Star led and guided them, but when they arrived in Jerusalem it apparently hid, unnoticed by anyone. After-wards, when they left Herod, it reappeared and led them southwards to Bethlehem to come to rest directly above the Child Messiah. This is not the behaviour of an astronomical body, but that of some guiding intelligence with a great purpose. It moved according to divine will: when they were to move, it led off and moved; when they were to stop, it stood and hid. When they arrived at their final destination, it departed. The Star had provided everything as needed, just like the pillar of cloud before the

---

[4] John Chrysostom, *Homilies on the Gospel of St Matthew*, Homily VI.

Israelites in the wilderness. It roused up the camp to move when necessary, at other times halting, giving direction and purpose to the new nation of Israel.

3

The Sequence
of Events

Let us piece together the sequence of events surrounding the Nativity and the appearance of the Star, from Luke's and Matthew's accounts:

1. In response to a Roman decree, Joseph had to go to his hometown of Bethlehem to be registered, and he took his pregnant wife with him. After they arrived, Mary came to term and needed somewhere to have the Baby.

2. It was late at night and there was no room at the inn, or with Joseph's family at such short notice, due to the incoming census population and the huge number of festival pilgrims taking all the available accommodation. So the innkeeper offered the stable, which was where Jesus was born. He was wrapped in swaddling clothes (tight wrappings around the Baby, such as is still practised in the

East) and laid in a manger (a trough from which animals normally fed).

3. That night there were shepherds in the surrounding fields, looking after the lambs destined for sacrifice in the Temple.

4. An angel of the Lord stood before them.

5. The Glory of the Lord shone around them.

6. The shepherds were greatly afraid, but the angel reassured them and then announced the birth of the Messiah. The angel also told them how to find the Child, and the sign would be that He would be found in a stable, in an animal's feeding trough.

7. Suddenly a great multitude of the heavenly host appeared, praising God.

8. The angel and the heavenly host finished their announcements and praises and returned to heaven.

9. The shepherds decided to go to Bethlehem and find the Messiah.

10. After they had found Him and seen Him, they made the entire experience widely known to anyone who would listen.

11. Everyone who heard it marvelled at what the shepherds had to say.

12. At the same time as the birth of the Messiah, Wise Men in the East saw His Star rising – the Glory of the Lord. They knew what it meant and decided to come to Judea to find this Messiah.

13. Meanwhile, after eight days, Jesus was circumcised according to the custom of the Jews, and given the name "Jesus", as the angel instructed.

14. After the days of her purification according to the Law of Moses were completed, Joseph and

Mary went to the Temple to dedicate Jesus as the firstborn male.

15. Joseph and Mary remained in Bethlehem until the mother and Child were able to undertake the arduous journey back to their home in Nazareth.

16. Some considerable time after these things occurred, and while Joseph and Mary still remained in Bethlehem, the Wise Men from the East arrived in Judea, looking for the Messiah, the King of the Jews.

17. Herod heard of it and he was troubled at this potential challenge to his throne.

18. He called together the chief priests and scribes and asked them where this Messiah was to be born. They told him in Bethlehem.

19. Herod called the Wise Men to him secretly, and found out from them when His Star had appeared.

20. Herod then told them they would find the Messiah in Bethlehem.

21. He sent the Wise Men off, asking them, once the Messiah was found, to tell him where to come.

22. Herod pretended eagerness to worship the Messiah. In reality he wanted to kill this perceived threat to his rule.

23. The Wise Men followed the king's instructions and departed for Bethlehem.

24. As they left Jerusalem, they were extremely glad to see His Star again, which they had originally seen in their homeland in the East.

25. The Star then appeared and went before them, leading them to the house where Jesus was with His mother, and stood over where the Child was.

26. They fell down and worshipped Him.

27. They gave Him presents of gold, frankincense and myrrh.

28. They were warned in a dream not to go back to Herod.

29. They left Judea by another route on the way home.

30. After the Wise Men had left, Joseph was warned in a dream to flee to Egypt, out of the reach of Herod.

31. Herod discovered he had been tricked by the Wise Men, and sent his soldiers to Bethlehem to kill the Messiah. Based on the information obtained from the Wise Men, Herod ordered all male children of the age of two years and under to be killed. Herod's murderous paranoia fulfilled the prophecy of Jeremiah:

A voice was heard in Ramah,
Lamentation and bitter weeping,
Rachel weeping for her children,
Refusing to be comforted for her children,
Because they are no more.

(Jeremiah 31:15)

With this sequence in mind, we can see that Jesus' birth in Bethlehem fulfilled Old Testament prophecy and began a New Covenant:

Behold, the days are coming, says the LORD, when I will make a new covenant with the house of Israel and with the house of Judah – not according to the covenant that I made with their fathers in the day that I took them by the hand to lead them out of the land of Egypt, My covenant which they broke, though I was a husband to them, says the LORD. But this is the covenant that I will make with the house of Israel after those days, says the LORD: I will put My law in their minds, and write it on their hearts; and I will be their God, and they shall be My people. No more shall every man teach his neighbor, and every man his brother, saying, "Know the LORD," for they all shall know Me, from the least of them to the greatest of them, says the LORD. For I will forgive their iniquity, and their sin I will remember no more.

(Jeremiah 31:31–34)

This passage refers to the New Covenant of grace, not the Old Covenant of the Law of Moses. This New Covenant will be written on the hearts of the believers and be constantly in their minds. The knowledge of the Lord will be freely available to anyone who desires it. Their sins will be forgiven and no longer remembered.

It is vital to know that this New Covenant is not just another version of the Old Covenant that God gave to the children of Israel at Sinai. It is radically different, not just a change in emphasis. It is not about a national legal system which tries to control behaviour, but about each person placing faith in the Lord and obtaining the forgiveness of sin, receiving a new heart, and with it, a new character. The foundation of the New Covenant is the work of Christ on the cross, and anyone who puts faith in Him shares in this New Covenant.

4

A Closer Look at the Star

If we read Matthew's account carefully, the "Star of Bethlehem" which the Magi saw is merely referred to as "His star". This would link with the Prophecy in Numbers 24:17 very well, since this is clearly a reference to Jesus Himself. Further, there is no Biblical evidence that the Star hovered over the stable where Jesus was born. The text says that it hovered over where Jesus was staying some time *after* his birth, when the Magi had arrived (Matthew 2:9–11). Luke's account is that the Glory of the Lord shone all around the shepherds at the time of Jesus' birth (Luke 2:9). This is probably what the Magi saw initially, before being inspired and led by a different manifestation of the Glory of the Lord.

The fact that Herod had to ask the Magi when the star first appeared perhaps means that the Star, the Glory of the Lord, was not visible to others. Only the shepherds, who were on the spot, and the Magi, some hundreds of miles away to the East, were aware of it. Why didn't the inhabitants of Bethlehem see it? Actually, if it was visible so far away, why didn't the people of Jerusalem and all the other cities in Judea see it? Thinking about it a little more, why wasn't the entire population of Judea blinded? The Star which attracted the Magi has no acceptable natural astronomical explanation. It was clearly a special sign miracle, signifying the birth of the Messiah, which put the fear of God into the shepherds and brought and guided the Magi from the East, yet left the inhabitants of Judea untouched. What could this be?

First, we must understand that God's Word was written down for those who weren't there, and especially for us because we live much later than the actual events. It is part of the purposes of God that we should know about these things. In that case, the Star of Bethlehem is an essential part of the story and we cannot ignore it. So what are we to make of it?

Initially, the Star led the Magi from *East to West*. When they arrived in Palestine, they made their way to King Herod. Having discovered the *time* of the birth of the prophesied Messiah from the Magi, Herod did his homework and asked the chief priests and scribes *where* this was prophesied to happen. He was told that it must be in Bethlehem according to the prophet Micah. So even though Scripture foretold the place of his birth, the time of it was revealed by a special sign miracle. This was new information to Herod and really caught his interest.

So Herod passed on this information about Bethlehem and sent the Magi there to act as his scouts, so he could kill the potential threat to his kingdom. When he found out he had been tricked, he flew into a rage and ordered the deaths of all male children there, from the age of two years and under. This gives us some idea of the lapse of time between the actual birth and the arrival of the Magi – up to one year and less than two years. Herod was being murderously thorough. Also, when Joseph was warned in a dream to take the Child to Egypt, to evade the deadly intent of Herod, the Child must have been old enough to survive the journey. A newborn infant would perish. The Scriptural account is so precisely realistic in every detail.

The last mention of the Star is when the Magi leave Herod on the last few miles of their journey, going south from Jerusalem to Bethlehem. This time the Star led them from *North to South*:

> ... the star which they had seen in the East went before them, till it came and stood over where the young Child was. When they saw the star, they rejoiced with exceedingly great joy.
>
> (Matthew 2:9–10)

In conclusion, the recorded behaviour of the Star is so peculiar that, if real, it can only be considered miraculous. The Scriptures do not contain errors of fact about such things, so we can be sure it is a miracle from God and not some kind of natural phenomenon.

There is no other mention of it. The Bible doesn't say that it left, or went out, or shot back up into the heavens. Nothing more is recorded. It was obviously real to the Magi, even if it could not be seen by others. This special miracle of the Star was visibly obvious to those who were wise in the knowledge of Scripture, and who trusted the prophecies enough to make a tremendous journey of faith to see the Messiah. There is perhaps a lesson for all of us here.

As Christians, we are to take this Star seriously. It is not just a nice story to charm the children. Nor is it something just to sing about in Christmas carols. It has a very important meaning and is a sign, first to the Jews and then to the Gentiles. It bridges the Old and New Testaments of the Bible. It is a sign of continuity that the God of Abraham, Isaac and Jacob is still in control of history. He keeps His promises, and is continually involved with the world in bringing His plans to completion. The Star can only be a manifestation of God Himself, His Glory shining out on the night of the birth of His Son, ennobling the lowly and summoning the wise. The Old Testament Shekinah Glory of God shone out in all its brilliance to signal the beginning of the New.

5

The Shekinah Glory of God

The Shekinah Glory of God is the visible manifestation of the presence of God. It is the awesome manifestation of the presence of the Lord where He comes down to dwell among men.[5] Whenever the transcendent, invisible and omnipresent God is localized for the benefit of us humans, there is the Shekinah Glory. The Old Testament Hebrew root of

---

[5] The Bible often refers to God dwelling with "men". This is an inclusive term meaning all the people of Israel, including women and children. When Paul wrote to the churches in the New Testament, he often began by addressing the "brethren" (cf. Romans 1:13). This is also an inclusive term, since he was writing to the whole church, including women and children. Whenever the words "men" or "Man" or "mankind" appear in this book, they are used in the same inclusive sense.

the word Shekinah is *Shakan*,[6] and has the meaning "to dwell". The New Testament Greek word *skeinei* means "to tabernacle". This gives us the full definition and meaning of the phrase, the Shekinah Glory of God, which is: the visible presence of God dwelling with men.

In the Old Testament, these manifestations usually took the form of light, fire or cloud, and sometimes deep darkness. In the New Testament there is a new example: Jesus our Messiah – God With Us – Emmanuel. We also have the light, fire and cloud in the New Testament, but more of that later.

One of the earliest and more obvious examples in the Old Testament is the story of Moses and the Burning Bush:

> Now Moses was tending the flock of Jethro his father-in-law, the priest of Midian. And he led the flock to the back of the desert, and came to Horeb, the mountain of God. And the Angel of the LORD appeared to him in a flame of fire from the midst of a bush. So he looked, and behold, the bush was burning with fire, but the bush was not consumed. Then Moses said, "I will now turn aside and see this great sight, why the bush does not burn."
>
> So when the LORD saw that he turned aside to

---

[6] *Shakan* (Strong's No 7931): to dwell. From nomadic life meaning to dwell in a tent. *Mishkan* (Strong's No 4908): dwelling place; tent. Often used for the Tabernacle of God in the wilderness. *Mishkan* was also used later to refer to the Temple in Jerusalem. This is the probable root of the word Shekinah, which was used to refer to the "presence" of God, or the presence of the Shekinah Glory of God. http://www.concordances.org/strongs.htm.

look, God called to him from the midst of the bush and said, "Moses, Moses!"

And he said, "Here I am."

Then He said, "Do not draw near this place. Take your sandals off your feet, for the place where you stand is holy ground." Moreover He said, "I am the God of your father – the God of Abraham, the God of Isaac, and the God of Jacob." And Moses hid his face, for he was afraid to look upon God.

(Exodus 3:1–6)

In these verses we are told that God showed Himself to Moses as the Angel of the Lord, in the form of fire as His visible presence. Most scholars of the Old Testament agree that the Angel of the Lord is the Second Person of the Trinity, the Son of God, the Messiah. When the Angel of the Lord appears, it is sometimes referred to as a Theophany or a Christophany. In this instance of the Burning Bush, it is the fire of the Shekinah Glory that commissions Moses to lead His people out of Egypt. This is recorded in the book of Exodus.

During the early part of the Exodus, God appeared as a pillar of fire by night and a column of smoke by day (Exodus 13:21–22). We also read, a little further on, that:

... the Angel of God, who went before the camp of Israel, moved and went behind them; and the pillar of cloud went from before them and stood behind them. So it came between the camp of the Egyptians and the camp of Israel. Thus it was a cloud and darkness to the one, and it gave light by night to the other, so that the one did not come near the other all that night.

(Exodus 14:19–20)

This not only held back Pharaoh and his army, it was also a sign that God was with them. Note the statement that it was the Angel of God which was manifested. This title is synonymous with the Angel of the Lord.

God was the means of their deliverance and salvation from the world – but only those who trusted Him were delivered. Pharaoh's heart was hardened against God and so he and his whole army perished in the Red Sea. Pharaoh was a symbol of worldly people who deny God, are evil continually, and perish in this world. If we go back even further, to a time when mankind was doing wickedness constantly, God swept them all away in a great flood which covered all the earth. Only Noah and his family survived on the ark.

It is only those who trust God for their deliverance and salvation who pass from this world through the waters of death (baptism) into the new life of the Promised Land, from this world into the next, from earth to heaven. Noah was a preacher of righteousness; only he and his family were saved. Everyone else drowned. Only the Israelites, led by Moses, trusted God, and were saved through the waters of the Red Sea. Pharaoh and his army drowned.

After the immediate danger from Pharaoh and Egypt had passed, God came to dwell with the Israelites in a tabernacle or tent. In the book of Exodus we find that Moses was commanded:

> And let them make Me a sanctuary, that I may dwell among them.
>
> (Exodus 25:8)

In the sanctuary, known as the Tabernacle, God dwelt in the Holy of Holies, above the Mercy Seat, which is the lid of the Ark of the Covenant containing the Law of God. The Holy of Holies was completely dark inside, because it was covered with six layers of materials of various kinds, to exclude all natural light. It was only the Shekinah Glory of God which provided the light, from His position above the Mercy Seat. This Shekinah Glory was the visible symbol of the presence of God. The story of the Tabernacle, its journeys with the Israelites, with King David, and the subsequent building of the Temple by Solomon, is contained in the writings of the Old Testament. It is a story full of triumphs and disasters, and it ends when God decides to leave.

The Israelites had become truly wicked, and did all the evil that God had forbidden them. God could no longer remain with them. The fullness of the iniquity of the Jews was complete; God then judged them and left. This is described in the book of Ezekiel, starting at chapter 10. God left the Holy of Holies, from above the cherubim on the Mercy Seat; He crossed the Holy Place and paused on the threshold of the Temple, where the court was filled with the brightness of the Glory of the Lord. Eventually, after the judgments on the wicked, the Shekinah Glory left the Temple and exited the city of Jerusalem by the East Gate, and crossed to the mountain on the east side of the city, the Mount of Olives. From there the Glory of God departed back to heaven. Due to the evildoing of His chosen people, the Shekinah Glory, symbolizing the presence of God with Man, had left. The brightness of His Glory left the sight of mankind. This was an absolute disaster, and subsequently the Israelites were taken into captivity in Babylon and the whole land was laid waste. The judgment of God had fallen on them.

Had God failed? Were the purposes of God thwarted? By no means. The devil is always trying to corrupt mankind and make them enemies of God like himself. It looked to him as though in this case he had actually succeeded with God's chosen people. The devil's eternal error is to think that God can ever be surprised, or His will overturned. God's will is definitive in the outcome of history. In this case, God left only to return in a more dramatic and significant way.

As we know from the book of Daniel, some of the righteous Jews in captivity in Babylon remained faithful to God. They continued to study the Scriptures and the prophecies of the coming Messiah-King. Daniel himself was probably instrumental in setting up schools, where the books of the Old Testament were studied and commented upon. These comments were the probable beginning of scholarship that was eventually brought together into what we know as the Talmud. This is the Jewish book of commentary on the Old Testament.[7] Later, after seventy years of captivity in Babylon, some of the Jews returned to Jerusalem and rebuilt the Temple and the city. The majority

---

[7] There are two versions of the Talmud: the Babylonian Talmud and the Jerusalem Talmud. The Babylonian is considered the superior, since it is older and more complete than the other. Compiled between the fourth century BC and the fifth century AD, it is written partly in Hebrew and partly in Aramaic. There are two parts to the Talmud, the *Mishna*, or text of the Oral Law (in Hebrew), and the *Gemara* (in Aramaic) which is a commentary on the *Mishna*. At the time of Christ, the Talmud was in its early stages of development. Nevertheless, these Magi, or Wise Men, would have studied the Old Testament prophecies and the very early commentaries about them. Almost certainly it was this wisdom and knowledge that brought the Magi to Israel, seeking the Messiah at the time and place of His prophecy.

remained in Babylon, where they were comfortable and assimilated. In this new Temple in a rebuilt Jerusalem, there was no Ark of the Covenant and no Shekinah Glory. The Holy of Holies was empty.

At the birth of Christ, more than 400 years later, the Wise Men, or Magi, came from the East seeking the Messiah-King. Many scholars have debated their origins, without coming to any clear decision. It is probable that they came from the tradition of the Jews who remained behind in Babylon, at the end of the Babylonian captivity. No doubt many continued their studies, and it is from these people that the Magi probably had their origin. We must realize that if the Star was visible from the East and the Star guided the Magi generally westwards towards Israel, we can assume they must have come out of Babylon or Persia, or from that general direction. These Wise Men were learned in the prophecies of the Messiah. Somehow they knew the time had come, and journeyed a long way. They recognized the signs of the times and knew the Star for what it was – the return of the Glory of God. If you remember the Scripture, the Glory of the Lord shone around the shepherds at the very moment of Christ's birth. This was the Shekinah Glory shining out to declare that God was once more dwelling with men.

It was this sign, the Shekinah Glory, manifested as a leading star, that they followed to Jerusalem and King Herod. It is a long journey from Babylon to Israel, and the Magi arrived, as we have already discussed, when Jesus was about a year old, or thereabouts. As mentioned above, Jesus and His family had long since left the stable, but were still residing in Bethlehem, and it was to this place that the Star subsequently led the Magi.

6

The Pascal Lamb

*I*t is worth pausing our narrative at this point and asking ourselves, what is the special significance of Bethlehem? We know that Bethlehem is associated with the House of David and the long line of the Messiah. In Micah 5:2 it is prophesied that the Messiah would be born there. In Hebrew, *Beth lehem* means "house of bread"; Jesus is the Bread of Heaven and we easily see the connection and God's touch in all this. But *lehem* also means "flesh" and was specifically applied to that part of the sacrifice[8] that was burnt on the altar. The word is also used to refer to a carcass.[9] So Bethlehem might more properly be

---

[8] Leviticus 3:11–16; 21:6.

[9] Zephaniah 1:17.

called the "house of flesh" or, as some scholars have suggested, "the house of the incarnation"; that is, the place where God became flesh for the salvation of the world.

But there is another significant factor, to do with the Temple sacrifices during the various feasts, especially Passover. There are three Jewish pilgrimage festivals with obligatory attendance. These are:

Pesach (*Passover*), 14 Nissan (late March – early April)
Shavuot (*Weeks*), (Christian Pentecost) 6 Sivan (late May – early June)
Sukkot (*Tabernacles* or *Booths*), 14–21 Tishri (late September – early October)

Every Jewish male had to go to the Temple during these three festivals, and frequently his family would go as well. Where possible they would stay with relatives; otherwise they would occupy rooms at the various inns, both in Jerusalem and the surrounding towns and villages, such as Bethlehem. Additionally, in this particular year, the census meant that many more people than usual would be in Bethlehem. This explains why the only accommodation for Joseph and his pregnant wife was a stable.

It has been estimated that about the time of the birth of Jesus, almost 300,000 lambs would need to be slaughtered at Passover each year, and many more throughout the religious calendar. Each of these animals had to be certified by the Temple priests to be without spot or blemish, symbolizing the sinlessness of the ultimate sacrifice of Jesus, the real Passover Lamb: *the* Lamb of God who takes away the sin of the world.

Obviously, the priests could not instantly inspect 300,000 lambs at one time. The solution was to inspect the lambs and store them somewhere until Passover, when each head of household could collect and slaughter his own lamb. Bethlehem was the place, and the shepherds who "watched their flocks by night",[10] as the Christmas carol has it, were the Temple shepherds responsible for the sacrificial lambs immediately before Passover. It was in this place that the ultimate Sacrificial Lamb was born,[11] in the springtime, among the actual Passover lambs awaiting sacrifice in any given year.

Do not be confused by the fact that in the West we celebrate the birth of Jesus on 25 December. In the fourth century AD when the Roman Empire came under Christian rule, the celebration of the Nativity was moved to 25 December in a bid to replace the Roman festival of Saturnalia, a pagan celebration in honour of the god Saturn, which had by then become an excuse for immoral behaviour. Originally, Saturnalia was a festival of light leading towards the winter solstice. Hundreds of candles were used, to symbolize human striving for knowledge and truth. The winter solstice on 25 December was celebrated as the *Dies Natalis* of *Sol Invictus*, or "The Birthday of the Unconquerable Sun". Perhaps the early church

---

[10] Nahum Tate (1652-1715), "While Shepherds Watched".

[11] Scholars hold different opinions as to the actual time of Jesus' birth; some say autumn at the Feast of Tabernacles, whereas others say springtime at the Feast of Passover. This author believes the evidence points to springtime and Passover for the historical First Coming, and autumn and Tabernacles for the prophesied Second Coming.

fathers wanted to replace the literal solar light with the radiance of God's Son, the true Light of the World. It's a nice thought.

The motivation for this move was a worthy one; unfortunately, moving the birth of Christ from the spring to midwinter has led to much distraction in the popular understanding of the birth of Jesus, His identity as the Messiah, as the Passover Lamb, and the significance of the Star of Bethlehem, the Shekinah Glory of God.

7

Just As We Are

$\mathcal{B}$efore we go back to the main narrative, there is one more thing which must be understood. Normally, in those days, shepherds would not tend large flocks near towns and villages. The smell of very large flocks was so bad that people could not stand the stench and may even have had difficulty breathing. This meant that large flocks were usually kept well out of the way, in areas far from centres of population.

However, Bethlehem was an exception. Once a year, for thirty days, an enormous flock of lambs, not less than eight weeks and not more than one year old, were allowed to graze near Bethlehem. This was the thirty days immediately before the Feast of Passover. Every lamb had been examined by the priests and declared unblemished. These were separated to be sacrificed as Passover lambs. The size of this flock required a large number of Temple shepherds, working around the clock in shifts. These would be the shepherds who saw the vision of the angels singing to the glory of God.

The area where the Temple shepherds watched the great flocks is in the valley south-east of Bethlehem. In the middle was a stone tower known as the *Migdal Eder* or the "Tower of the Flock". This tower was used by the priests who oversaw the shepherds. By staying in it, the priests kept themselves from becoming ritually defiled. The book of Leviticus describes how this could happen; one of the ways was by coming into contact with faeces or dead things. When such defilement occurred, purification rites had to be strictly observed. In a society which took these things seriously, shepherds were shunned because they were never clean. It was impossible. They were constantly walking about in sheep excrement and touching dead things, and both left them in a state of ritual impurity.

Because of their defiled condition, shepherds were not normally allowed into the Temple to offer sacrifices, or into the synagogues on the Sabbath. So even though they were Jewish, they were excluded from worshipping God according to the Law of Moses. Also, according to the religious authorities of the day, the idea of worshipping God apart from the Temple was impossible. So even the most pious shepherds were labelled as being unclean, and could not therefore come into the presence of God. Yet it would be these unclean, ritually defiled shepherds of Bethlehem whom God would call to be the first to visit His Son.

The priests and scribes, Pharisees and Sadducees alike, would find it unbelievable for God to do this. Bethlehem shepherds were the last people that God should assign to this task. They would assume that God would send some of their own kind, who could be found in the Temple. They thought they knew everything there was to know about God. After all, their sacred traditions came directly from God and they kept themselves ritually clean. So they believed that they were righteous. They were the religious professionals and presumed that they were far godlier than these defiled shepherds. Sadly, their religion and religious practices had become a form of self-righteousness which left God out of the equation. They were unaware of this failing – they were proud of their religion. So, these people may have been doing everything right in an external sense, but humility was missing. They had no real love for their God or their neighbours. They were simply doing their religious ritual formulas and missing the main point.

One of the titles God takes to Himself in the Old Testament is "The Shepherd of Israel" or "The Great Shepherd". King David started out as a shepherd until God raised him to be king of all Israel. Jesus Himself, during His ministry, told the parable of the Good Shepherd, likening Himself to a shepherd who would go to any lengths to save just one sheep of His flock. Jesus was also reminding His hearers that He was "The Shepherd of Israel", one of the titles of God Himself. How the proud always miss the point.

Praise God that He chose to invite the shepherds, the lowest of the low and the outcasts of society, to the birth of His Son. Don't miss the significance of this tiny part of God's Word. It tells us that the least among us, the outcasts and the nobodies, are invited and are able to meet Him. There are no complicated rituals and no one is excluded. We do not need to be priests or theologians or have worldly status to begin this relationship; we must simply be willing to come to Him as we are, in faith.

8

The Wise Men and Their Gifts

$\mathcal{G}$oing back to our narrative, the Wise Men arrived at Jerusalem and we can deduce that the Star was no longer in evidence. This may explain why they went to see King Herod, possibly for help regarding where to go next, since they could not see the Star at this point. There was perhaps a deeper purpose, where this visit would ensure that the ruler of Israel was fully informed about the birth of the Messiah. We can only assume that, for His reasons, God wanted King Herod to know, otherwise the Star would have taken them straight to Jesus; a visit to Herod was not needed. Why would God want Herod to know? Because, as the current king of Israel, Herod was being told that the *real* King of Israel was here; the Old Covenant and the Law of Moses were being supplanted by a New Covenant. We know how Herod responded.

Did you notice that no one went with the Wise

Men from Herod's court? Not one member of God's elect people went with them to see the Messiah. These Gentile foreigners had journeyed a tremendous distance, but no Jew had the simple good manners to accompany them on the last few miles of their quest. The rejection of Jesus began at His birth.

The Wise Men left King Herod, and the Star reappeared and led them precisely to where Jesus lay. We can only wonder about their feelings when they saw the Star again. Matthew 2:10 describes how: "When they saw the star, they rejoiced with exceedingly great joy." Their supernatural guide had returned. It was clear to them what the Star signified and who this Child was: the Star stood over the young Child and they worshipped Him. The Star was nothing less than the Glory of God, come to earth to show the arrival of the Messiah, the Son of God. The Shekinah Glory, the Old Testament symbol of the presence of the Lord, had returned to guide the Wise Men to the actual Lord who would dwell among men from now on.

Then the Wise Men presented their gifts: gold to signify the eternal King; frankincense to signify His deity; and myrrh for anointing unto death of the Passover Lamb. They knew what they were doing and Who this Child was. The Christmas carol "We Three Kings" tells of these three gifts and what they signify. Sadly, we don't teach our children the proper significance of the Star or the gifts. We perpetuate the misleading iconic images of shepherds, the manger and the animals. We persist in saying "kings" instead of the true translation of Magi which is "Wise Men".

After the Wise Men enter the dwelling to worship Jesus, the Star is no longer in sight and is never mentioned again. The Old Testament Shekinah Glory, signifying the presence of God dwelling or living with Man, had completed the job of introducing the Wise Men to the incarnation of God in Jesus Christ – Emmanuel: God With Us.

> In the beginning was the Word, and the Word was with God, and the Word was God.
>
> (John 1:1)

> And the Word became flesh and dwelt among us, and we beheld His glory …
>
> (John 1:14)

The word translated "dwelt" is the Greek word *skeinei*, which literally means "to tabernacle", as we saw before. There is another Greek word which means to dwell. So John 1:14 should be literally translated as "And the Word became flesh and *tabernacled* among us." In other words, this was the new visible manifestation of the presence of God dwelling among men.

There is a striking parallel to the Old Testament that should not be missed. Originally, the Shekinah Glory (sometimes as the Angel of the Lord) came and went, but eventually stayed to dwell in the Tabernacle and Temple. It departed from the Mount of Olives. In the New Testament it appeared and disappeared, then stayed to dwell on earth in the human form of Jesus the Messiah. After His public ministry was complete, He also departed from the Mount of Olives.

9

The Shekinah Glory in the New Testament

$\mathcal{W}$e have already looked at the first two appearances of the Shekinah Glory: the appearance to the shepherds, where the Glory of the Lord shone around them; and the appearance to the Magi, as a guiding Star. I would like to look at three other instances, just to demonstrate that this approach is solidly founded in Scripture, and especially in the New Testament.

THE TRANSFIGURATION

Jesus took three of His disciples to the top of the Mount of Olives for His Transfiguration – a display of God's Glory in the person of His Son, Jesus Christ (Matthew 17:1–8; Mark 9:2–8; Luke 9:28–36). We don't know exactly how He looked to the disciples, but we know His face was as bright as the sun and His clothes changed to a whiteness impossible for human achievement.

Moses and Elijah appeared also. Both of these are Old Testament figures. Peter offered to make three tabernacles – one for Jesus, one for Moses, and one for Elijah. He may have been thinking that the Jews would have a final great celebration of the Feast of Tabernacles now that the Messiah had come. However, he didn't know what he was doing, because Jesus still had to go to the cross.

During the Transfiguration, a cloud overshadowed Jesus. This has symbolic and prophetic significance as well as historical reference. We have both the brightness and the cloud. It is first a reminder of the past appearance of God to Moses on Mount Sinai (Exodus 24), when God also spoke from a cloud. At the same time, there are hints of the Second Coming: Jesus will come with clouds, suddenly revealed as God's Messiah, and will stand on the Mount of Olives. Jewish tradition has always associated the Feast of Tabernacles with the coming of the Messiah, as well as with the journey in the wilderness after the Exodus. This probably explains Peter's desire to build three tabernacles. The Jews still reject Jesus as the Messiah; which is why they will not recognize His First Coming at the Feast of Passover. They are still looking for His First Coming at Tabernacles, whereas all true Christians (made up of saved Gentiles and saved Jews) are expecting Him then for the second time. The Transfiguration ends with God's voice speaking from the cloud, as it does in Exodus. (See Exodus 19:16-19; 24:16; 33:9.)The disciples heard that Jesus was God's beloved Son, the chosen one with whom He was well pleased.

The Transfiguration of Jesus is a manifestation of God's Glory, normally hidden behind His human form. It is a reminder of the Old Testament, but at the same time is much greater because it is a demonstration of the divine nature of Jesus, simultaneously both man and God. The face of Moses shone with reflected glory, whereas Jesus' face shone as the Shekinah Glory itself. Peter later wrote in his second letter:

> For we did not follow cunningly devised fables when we made known to you the power and coming of our Lord Jesus Christ, but were eyewitnesses of His majesty. For He received from God the Father honor and glory when such a voice came to Him from the Excellent Glory: "This is My beloved Son, in whom I am well pleased." And we heard this voice which came from heaven when we were with Him on the holy mountain.
>
> (2 Peter 1:16–18)

Peter was confirming that they weren't making this up. Jesus truly was King and Messiah.

There are other parts of the New Testament in which this new manifestation of the Glory of God is confirmed. Paul wrote:

> For God, who said, "Let light shine out of darkness," made his light shine in our hearts to give us the light of the knowledge of the glory of God in the face of Christ.
>
> (2 Corinthians 4:6 NIV1984)

Through Jesus, light shines out of a great darkness, and Paul is explaining that this light is the knowledge of the Glory of God, as seen in the face of Jesus Himself.

THE DAY OF PENTECOST

In the book of Acts, the Day of Pentecost brought a miraculous manifestation of the Glory of God:

> When the Day of Pentecost had fully come, they were all with one accord in one place. And suddenly there came a sound from heaven, as of a rushing mighty wind, and it filled the whole house where they were sitting. Then there appeared to them divided tongues, as of fire, and one sat upon each of them.
>
> (Acts 2:1–3)

This appearance of the tongues of fire is a manifestation of the Shekinah Glory which, as we noted before, often appears as fire. This is also closely associated with the Holy Spirit filling the disciples, with the purpose of fitting them for future ministry. It is confirmation that, as Jesus promised, He would send a Helper after He ascended back to heaven. So we can see that true disciples of Christ have the Holy Spirit, the Glory of God Himself, dwelling within them. This is yet another new way of God dwelling with all those who accept Him.

ON THE DAMASCUS ROAD

There is one occurrence of the appearance of the Shekinah Glory in the New Testament that is really obvious: the experience of Paul on the road to Damascus.

> As he journeyed he came near Damascus, and suddenly a light shone around him from heaven. Then he fell to the ground, and heard

a voice saying to him, "Saul, Saul, why are you persecuting Me?"

And he said, "Who are You, Lord?"

Then the Lord said, "I am Jesus, whom you are persecuting. It is hard for you to kick against the goads."

So he, trembling and astonished, said, "Lord, what do You want me to do?"

Then the Lord said to him, "Arise and go into the city, and you will be told what you must do."

And the men who journeyed with him stood speechless, hearing a voice but seeing no one. Then Saul arose from the ground, and when his eyes were opened he saw no one. But they led him by the hand and brought him into Damascus. And he was three days without sight, and neither ate nor drank.

(Acts 9:3–9)

The Glory of God is described in this passage as a light shining out of heaven. Paul was blinded for three days. After the three days in darkness, Ananias came at the prompting of the Lord and restored his sight – a figurative death and rebirth. Paul was filled with the Holy Spirit, then went away to consider his ways and repent. The purpose of this manifestation of the Glory was to identify and anoint Paul as the Apostle to the Gentiles:

But the Lord said to him [Ananias], "Go, for he is a chosen vessel of Mine to bear My name before Gentiles, kings, and the children of Israel. For I will show him how many things he must suffer for My name's sake."

(Acts 9:15–16)

We can see another example in the book of Revelation, where Jesus appears to the Apostle John undisguised in His glorified body:

> Then I turned to see the voice that spoke with me. And having turned I saw seven golden lampstands, and in the midst of the seven lampstands One like the Son of Man, clothed with a garment down to the feet and girded about the chest with a golden band. His head and hair were white like wool, as white as snow, and His eyes like a flame of fire; His feet were like fine brass, as if refined in a furnace, and His voice as the sound of many waters; He had in His right hand seven stars, out of His mouth went a sharp two-edged sword, and His countenance was like the sun shining in its strength.
>
> (Revelation 1:12–16)

The Glory of God is here no longer veiled in Jesus' human form. His face shines brighter than the sun. He is now in the fullness of His Glory. The purpose of this final appearance was to cause John to write the book of Revelation, and so bring Scripture to a close.

10

A Reflection of His Glory

When we read the book of Exodus in the Old Testament we read of Moses' face shining with the reflected Glory of God after his forty day sojourn with Him on Mount Sinai (Exodus 34:28–35). Moses later wore a veil over his face to conceal the radiance. Whenever he went in to be with the Lord face to face, Moses removed the veil; and when he came out to the children of Israel, he replaced the veil. The veil was there because the children of Israel were afraid of the Glory, and also because the veil concealed the fading of the Glory until the next time Moses went in to the Lord, when it would be renewed.

Moses reflected the Glory of the Lord for a time, after God manifested Himself in His Shekinah Glory. Modern believers today can also reflect the Glory of the Messiah, Jesus Christ, who was, and is, an even greater manifestation of that Glory. Consider the writing of Paul:

> Therefore, since we have such hope, we use great boldness of speech – unlike Moses, who put a veil over his face so that the children of Israel could not look steadily at the end of what was passing away. But their minds were blinded. For until this day the same veil remains unlifted in the reading of the Old Testament, because the veil is taken away in Christ. But even to this day, when Moses is read, a veil lies on their heart. Nevertheless when one turns to the Lord, the veil is taken away. Now the Lord is the Spirit; and where the Spirit of the Lord is, there is liberty. But we all, with unveiled face, beholding as in a mirror the glory of the Lord, are being transformed into the same image from glory to glory, just as by the Spirit of the Lord.
>
> (2 Corinthians 3:12–18)

In his second letter to the Corinthians, Paul is here referring to the passage in Exodus we have just discussed, and using the imagery there to make his point. The face of Moses was veiled to hide the fading of the Glory. This veil still remains on the heart of Israel, who has failed to see the passing away of the Law of the Old Covenant. When Moses turned to the Lord, the veil was removed. In the same way, when a believer (Jew or Gentile) turns to the Lord Jesus, the veil is removed and it becomes possible for the manifest Glory of the Lord to be reflected in the believer. Paul deals with this in verse 18, explaining that we look on Jesus, the Glory of the Lord, without a veil, and we are being transformed into the same image by the Spirit of the Lord. The Glory seen in the Messiah creates a dependent glory in the believer. It must be emphasized that the glory of the earthly believer is dependent glory, and is manifest in us only as long as we look on Jesus and obey His commands. If we look away, it fades.

The most striking image Paul uses here is the mirror. He says that we are beholding the Glory of the Lord as in a mirror. What do we see in a mirror? Ourselves! Make no mistake, it is Jesus who is the Shekinah Glory, and the believer should reflect that Glory. That is why Paul uses the idea of the mirror. By analogy, Jesus is the sun and the believer is the moon; the sun shines but the moon reflects. In the case of Moses, this reflection was shown in the shining of his face. For the believer, this reflection should be seen in the transforming of the believer's life and behaviour. As we have shown, the Glory is connected with the Holy Spirit, and it is the Holy Spirit which is now instrumental in effecting the changes in a believer's life "from glory to glory".

Did you ever wonder what the phrase "the praise of His glory" meant? In the opening section of Paul's letter to the Ephesians, Paul writes that we are called to holiness and adoption in Him, and in verse 6, "to *the praise of the glory of His grace*"; and in verse 12, "… we who first trusted in Christ should be to *the praise of His glory.*" Also in verses 13 and 14, he writes: "… you were sealed with the Holy Spirit of promise, who is the guarantee of our inheritance until the redemption of the purchased possession, to *the praise of His glory.*" (My emphasis throughout.)

"The praise of His glory" is simply a way of describing how we are being changed until the day of our final salvation arrives. Our attitude, obedience and behaviour is the reflection and praise of the glory that He shares with us through our faith in Him. I would like to close this discussion by simply quoting Paul's prayer for spiritual wisdom:

Therefore I also, after I heard of your faith in the Lord Jesus and your love for all the saints, do not cease to give thanks for you, making mention of you in my prayers: that the God of our Lord Jesus Christ, the Father of glory, may give to you the spirit of wisdom and revelation in the knowledge of Him, the eyes of your understanding being enlightened; that you may know what is the hope of His calling, what are *the riches of the glory of His inheritance in the saints,* and what is the exceeding greatness of His power toward us who believe, according to the working of His mighty power which He worked in Christ when He raised Him from the dead and seated Him at His right hand in the heavenly places, far above all principality and power and might and dominion, and every name that is named, not only in this age but also in that which is to come.

(Ephesians 1:15–21, my emphasis)

11

The Second Coming

We have been looking at the Real Star of Bethlehem and discovered that it was a manifestation of the Shekinah Glory of God, which first appears very early in the Old Testament. One of the historical purposes of God in manifesting His Glory in this way, was to announce the First Coming – the birth of the Messiah.

One of the great desires we all have is to know about the Second Coming of Christ. Questions such as: "When will it happen?" and "What will it be like?" have always been discussed among believers. There are many passages in the Bible which describe that great day, but we are discussing the Star of Bethlehem as the Shekinah Glory of God, which announced the First Coming and pointed the way from the Old to the New Covenants. The announcement of the Second Coming is reported in three places in the New Testament. In each case it is Jesus Himself who speaks:

For the Son of Man will come in the glory of His

Father with His angels, and then He will reward
each according to his works.

(Matthew 16:27)

Then they will see the Son of Man coming in the
clouds with great power and glory.

(Mark 13:26)

Then they will see the Son of Man coming in a
cloud with power and great glory.

(Luke 21:27)

We read that the Son of Man will come in the "glory
of His Father" and will be seen again, this time by the
entire world. He will be seen in the clouds with great
power and glory. This is confirmed in another verse
from Matthew:

Then the sign of the Son of Man will appear in
heaven, and then all the tribes of the earth will
mourn, and they will see the Son of Man coming
on the clouds of heaven with power and great glory.

(Matthew 24:30)

The sign of the Son of Man in the clouds of heaven
with great glory is the Shekinah Glory of God, which
has appeared at key points in history throughout the
entire Bible, and will announce the Second Coming,
as it did the First Coming. The manifestation of God's
Glory is different in each case, but it is the same Glory,
acting throughout history, as the visible sign of His
involvement and compassion, that all should come
to the Glory of God and His salvation, and that none
should perish.

Epilogue

The Continuity of History and God's Plan of Salvation

The existence of the Star in the Bible narrative is not an incidental detail. Nor is it an astronomical body or a literary invention. There is a profound and eternal purpose to the Star, a manifestation of the Glory of God, signifying that the God of Abraham, Isaac and Jacob would once more dwell among us. Matthew's Gospel begins the New Testament with the words: "The book of the genealogy of Jesus Christ, the Son of David, the Son of Abraham …" The Star is the symbol of continuity from the Old Testament to the New. The Star above the Child is saying, "Pay attention! This is My Son. We are One."

This was the will of God: that the Angel of the Lord, the Second Person of the Trinity, the Shekinah Glory, His only Son, would come from heaven and die as atonement for sin, be crucified, and be buried as a truly dead human being. On the third day God raised Him back to life; after forty days Jesus returned to heaven, bodily personified. One day He will return as Judge and King. God has given Him all authority in heaven and on earth.

Since the ascension of Jesus back to heaven, we are living in the church age, where the Holy Spirit dwells with every believer – once more God tabernacles with Man. It is through Jesus that we all may be reconciled to God. His sacrifice as the Passover Lamb atones for our sins and brings forgiveness and salvation. After that, God can live with each one of us through the Holy Spirit. Since the death and resurrection of Christ, God truly dwells with every believer.

God dwelt with Adam and Eve in the Garden of Eden. After the Fall, God could not dwell with sinful people. However, He has always had a plan to set things right and return us to innocence and to living with Him. This is the long story of the Israelites as God's chosen people, culminating in the First Coming of Jesus as the Suffering Servant, foretold by the great prophet Isaiah. In this plan of God, the whole earth is blessed through His Son, Jesus Christ: who is the radiance and brightness of the Glory of God (see Hebrews 1:1–3).

At the end of this age, Jesus will return as the King in judgment, and ultimately this earth will pass away, and a new earth and new heaven will be recreated for us to dwell together with God for eternity. The book of Revelation explains:

> And I heard a loud voice from heaven saying, "Behold, the tabernacle of God is with men, and He will dwell with them, and they shall be His

people. God Himself will be with them and be their God."

(Revelation 21:3)

The Star of Bethlehem shows us the way to the Living Lord, who is the same yesterday, today and tomorrow. Wise people will find Him, and bring the gifts of their lives in the service of the one true and Living God, in a reflection of His Glory, from glory to glory, and dwell with Him forever.

Suggested Further Reading

Alfred Edersheim, *The Life and Times of Jesus the Messiah* (Peabody, MA: Hendrickson Publishers, 1993).

Alfred Edersheim, *The Temple – Its Ministry and Services* (Peabody, MA: Hendrickson Publishers, 1994).

Arnold G. Fruchtenbaum, *The Footsteps of the Messiah* Appendix IV (San Antonio, TX: Ariel Ministries, 2003).

Matthew Henry, *Commentary on the Whole Bible* (Peabody, MA: Hendrickson Publishers, 1991).

Patrick Moore, *The Star of Bethlehem* (Bristol: Canopus Publishing, 2001).

Warren W. Wiersbe, *The Bible Exposition Commentary* (Colorado Springs, CO: Victor Books, an imprint of Cook Communications Ministries, 2002).

NOTES:
There are many sceptical books about the Star of

Bethlehem, based on astronomy, astrology, and many other topics. A quick search of the major booksellers on the Internet will show this. I chose the book by Patrick Moore as an engaging and fair account of the astronomical approach to the Star. There are many other books on the subject, but reader discretion is advised, since some amazing theories are cloaked in pseudo-scientific methods. Handle with care!

Finally, the Bible commentaries mentioned above are primarily relevant to chapter 2 of both Matthew and Luke, as far as the subject of the Star of Bethlehem is concerned. However, they are also useful (and necessary) for looking into the prophecies of the Messiah.

About the Author

Arthur Green served in the British Army for fifteen years, and came to faith together with his wife through their local Baptist church in the early 1990s. Arthur has worked in business and set up his own consultancy company in 1996, which he still operates together with his work as the CEO of Breakthrough to People Network in Georgia, USA. Arthur also co-ordinates the work of a small UK-based charity which provides development for educational facilities in India.

Arthur spent time as a development worker in the Middle East and Europe, followed by some years working as a humanitarian worker in the Sudan and other countries. The author's witnessing of the fall of communism, the suffering of people of many ideologies and religions under natural or man-made disasters, and the aftermath of wars produced a soul-searching examination of Arthur's Christian faith. The emptiness of life in the West which removed a sense of destiny from so many people in Western nations has been accompanied by a rising tide of violence and moral degeneration. Arthur has another book published by Sovereign World, *When Fables Fall*, which is an exposition of the decline of Christianity in the West, which has been the source of so many freedoms we now take for granted. The book examines the reasons behind the rise of evolution theory and humanistic philosophy which is attempting to usurp our Christian faith.

Also by Arthur Francis Green:

WHEN FABLES FALL
Unmasking the lies of distorted science, secularism and humanism

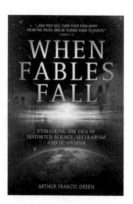

£10.99 / 240pp / 978 1 85240 593 9 / Sovereign World Ltd

We hope you enjoyed reading this Sovereign
World book. For more details of other
Sovereign
books and new releases see our website:

www.sovereignworld.com

Find us on Twitter @sovereignworld

Our authors welcome your feedback on their books.
Please send your comments to our offices.
You can request to subscribe to
our email and mailing list online or by writing to:

**Sovereign World Ltd, PO Box 784,
Ellel, Lancaster, LA1 9DA, United Kingdom
info@sovereignworld.com**

Sovereign World titles are available from
all good Christian bookshops and eBook vendors.

For information about our distributors in the UK,
USA, Canada, South Africa, Australia and Singapore, visit:
www.sovereignworld.com/trade

Sovereign World Trust, PO Box 777,
Tonbridge, Kent TN11 0ZS
United Kingdom

www.sovereignworldtrust.org.uk

The Sovereign World Trust is a registered charity